WOMEN WHO FINISH

THE FOCUS NOTEBOOK

WomenWhoFinish.com

"But I do not account my life of any value nor as precious to myself, **if only I may finish my course** and the ministry that I received from the Lord Jesus."

– Acts 20:24

BUT FIRST, FOCUS.

DROP ALL DISTRACTIONS

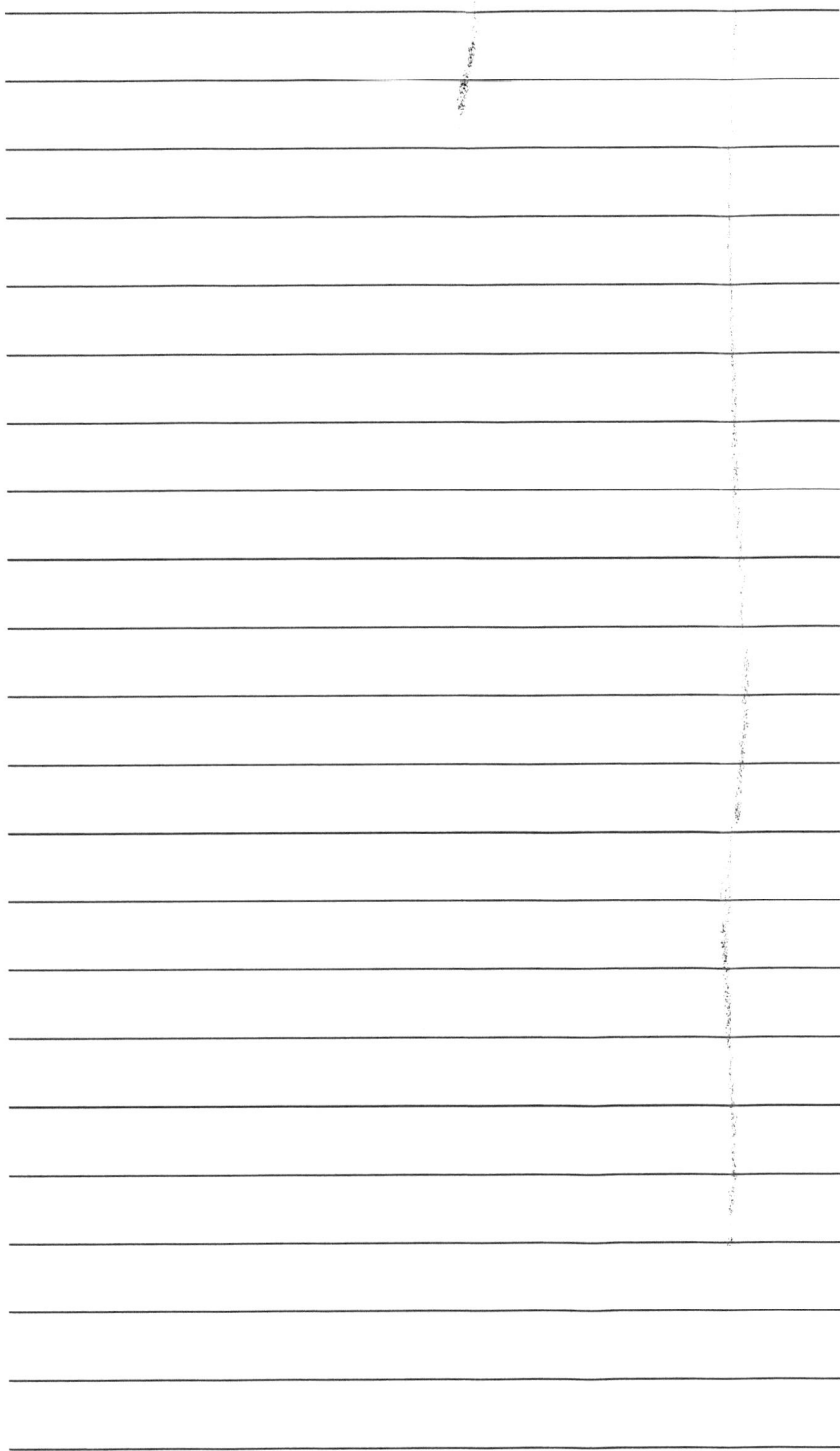

DREAM.
DECIDE.
DO.

REMEMBER
WHY
YOU
STARTED

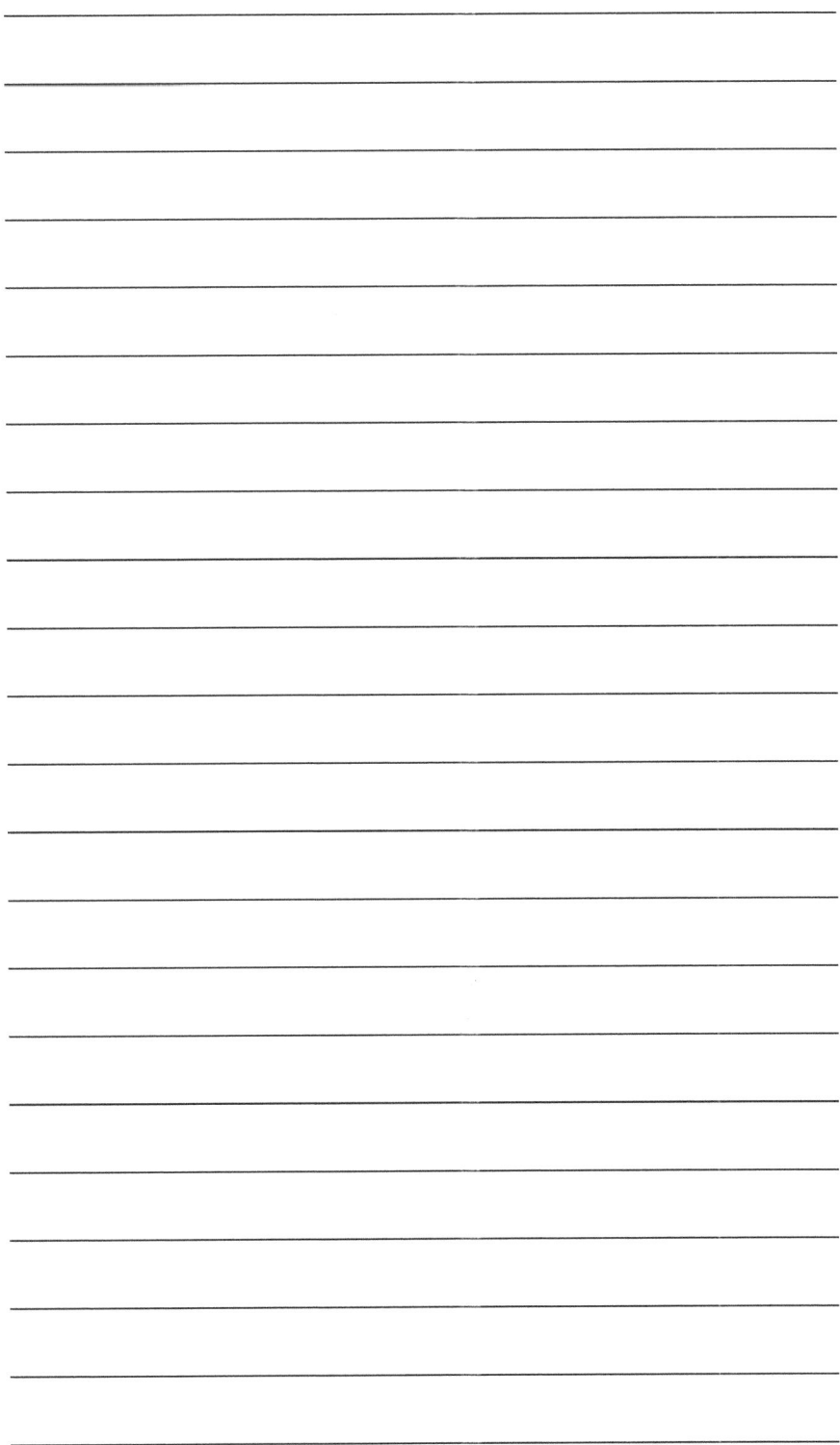

BECAUSE YOU SAID YOU WOULD.

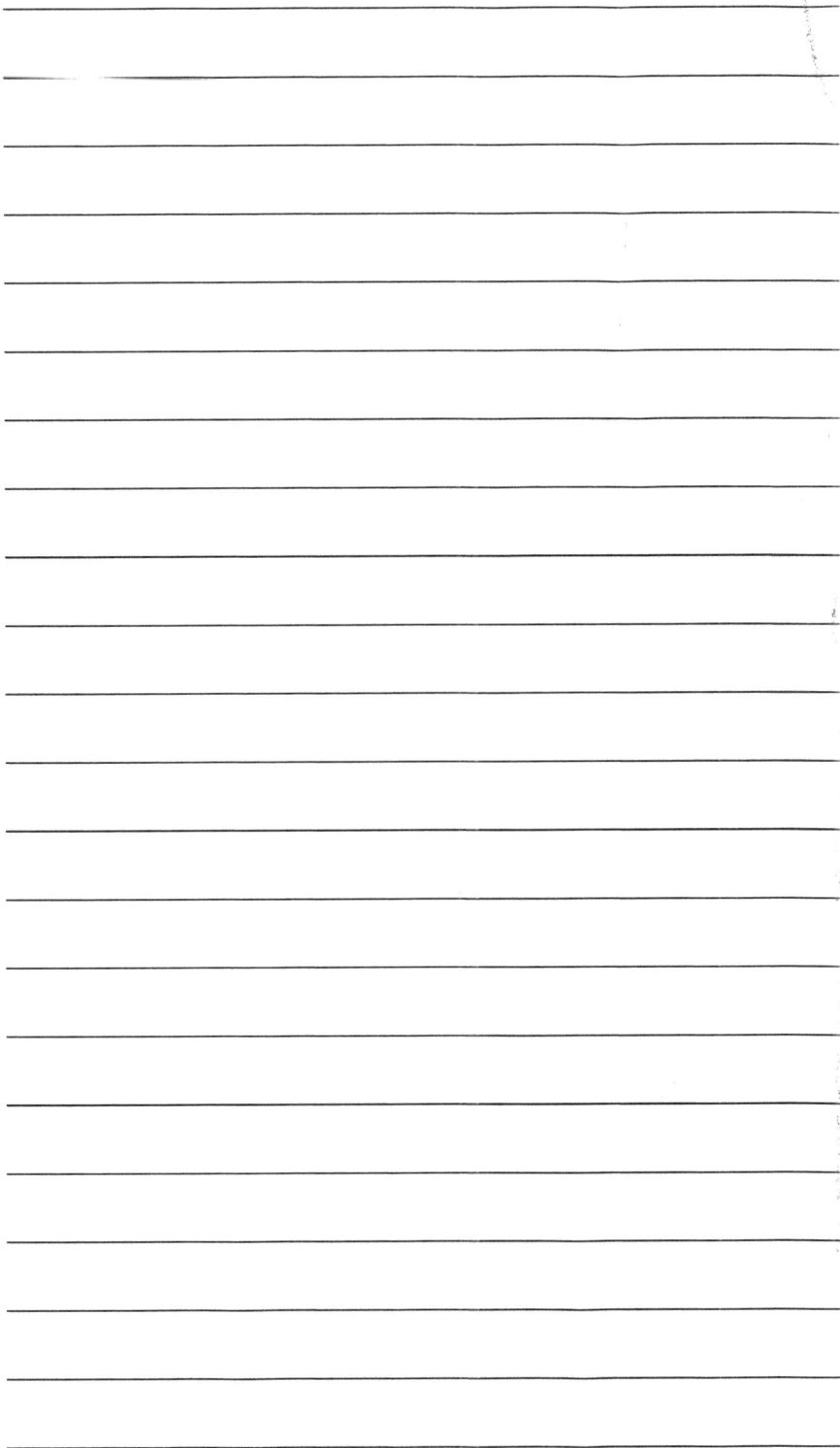

DON'T JUST PLAN TO START, PLAN TO FINISH.

PRIORITIZE YOUR CALLING.

FEEL FREE
TO
REFOCUS.

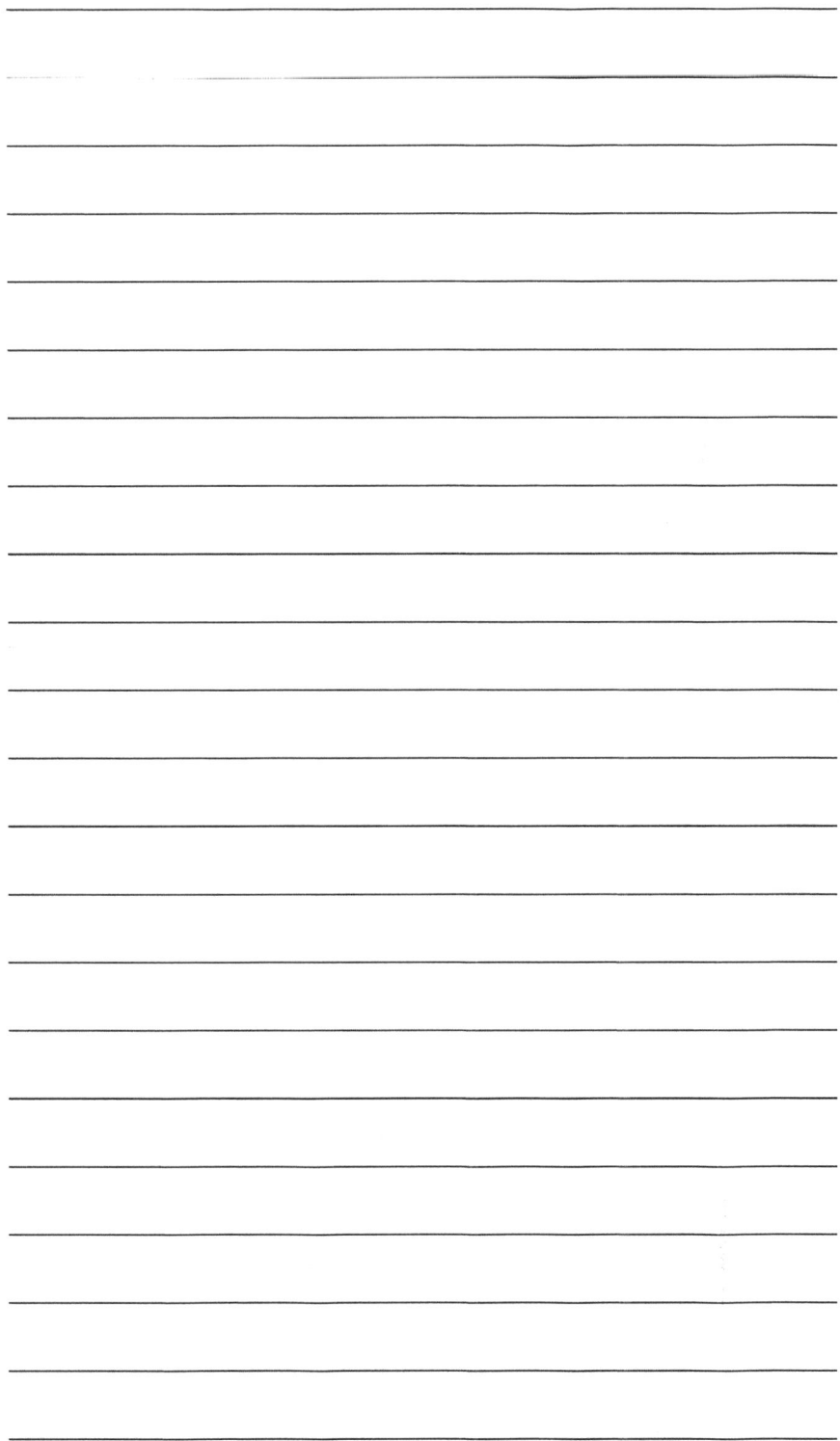

KEEP THE MAIN THING THE MAIN THING.

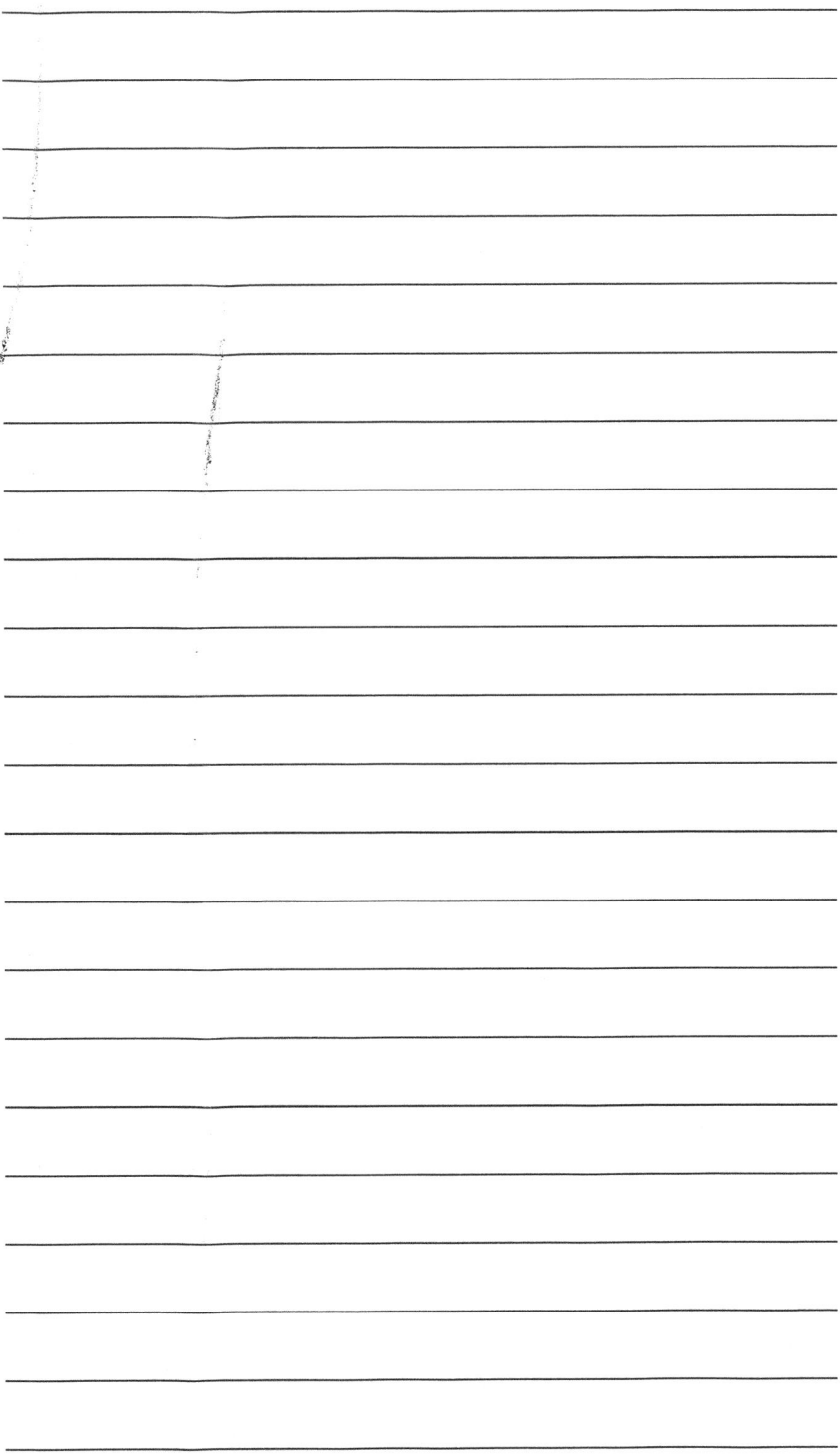

DISCIPLINE, KEEPING THE PROMISES YOU MADE TO YOURSELF.

MAKE TODAY MATTER.

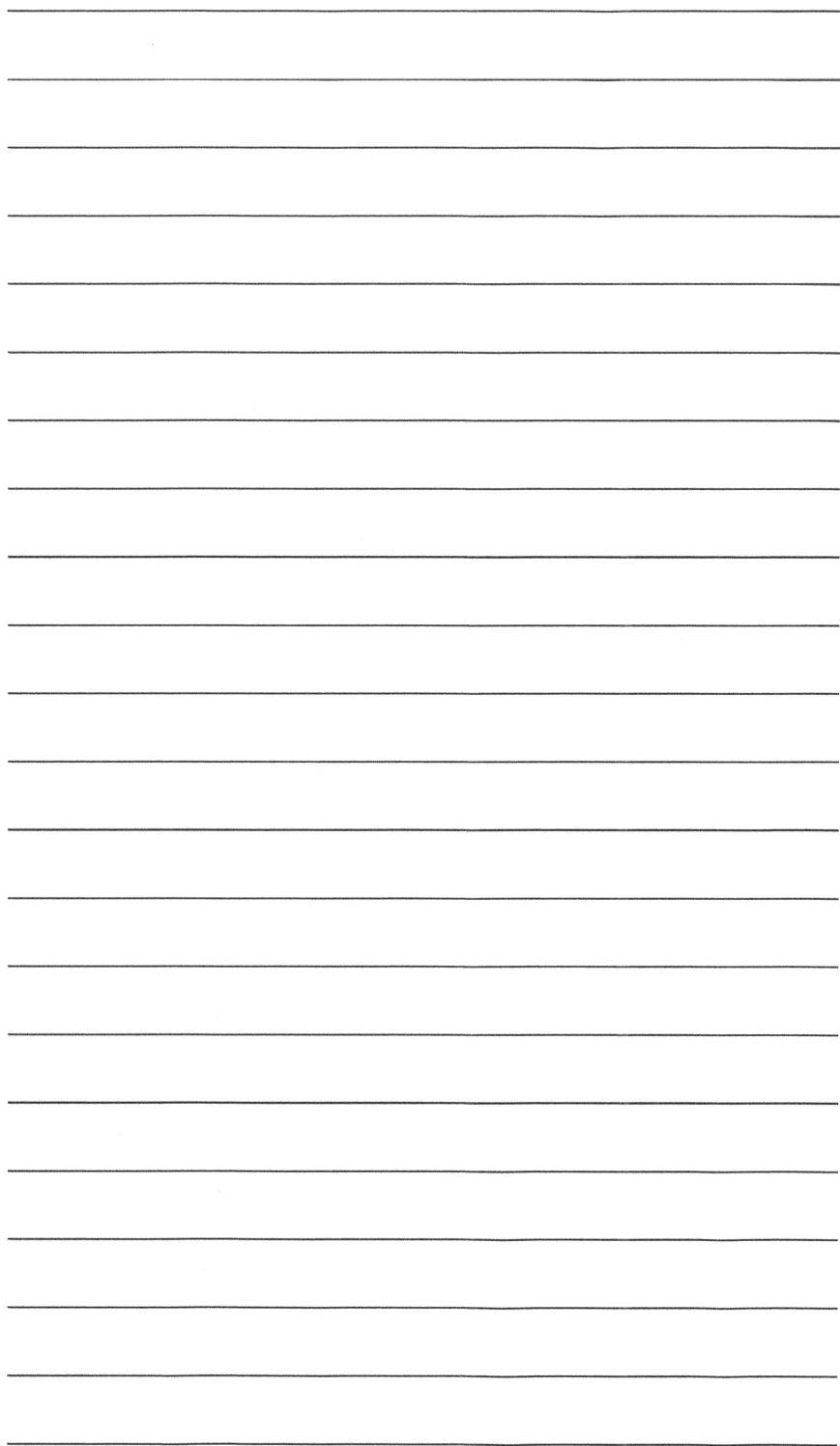

NEW
WEEK
RESOLUTIONS
ALLOWED.
START
AGAIN.

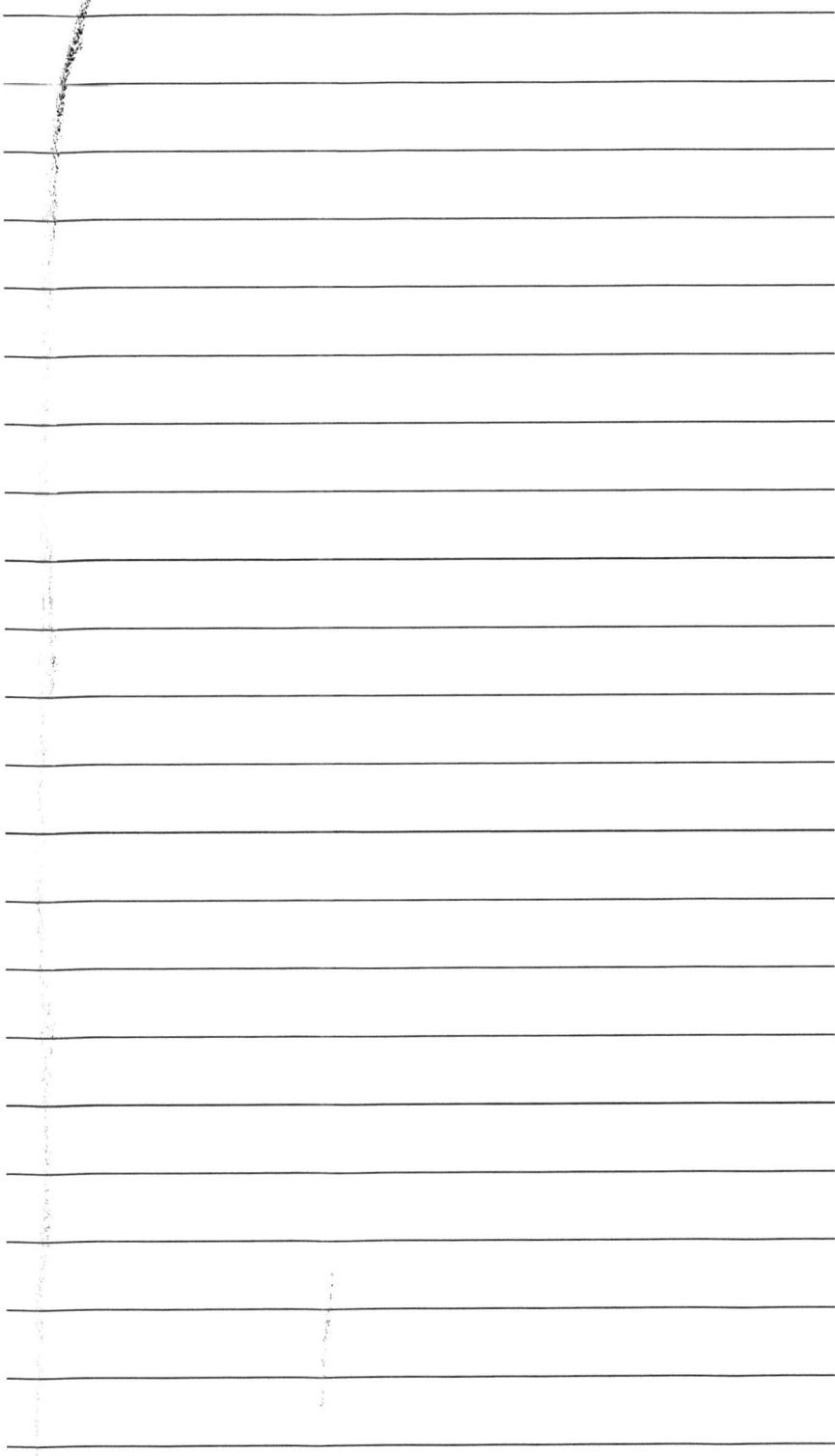

WRITE
THE
VISION,
MAKE
IT PLAIN.

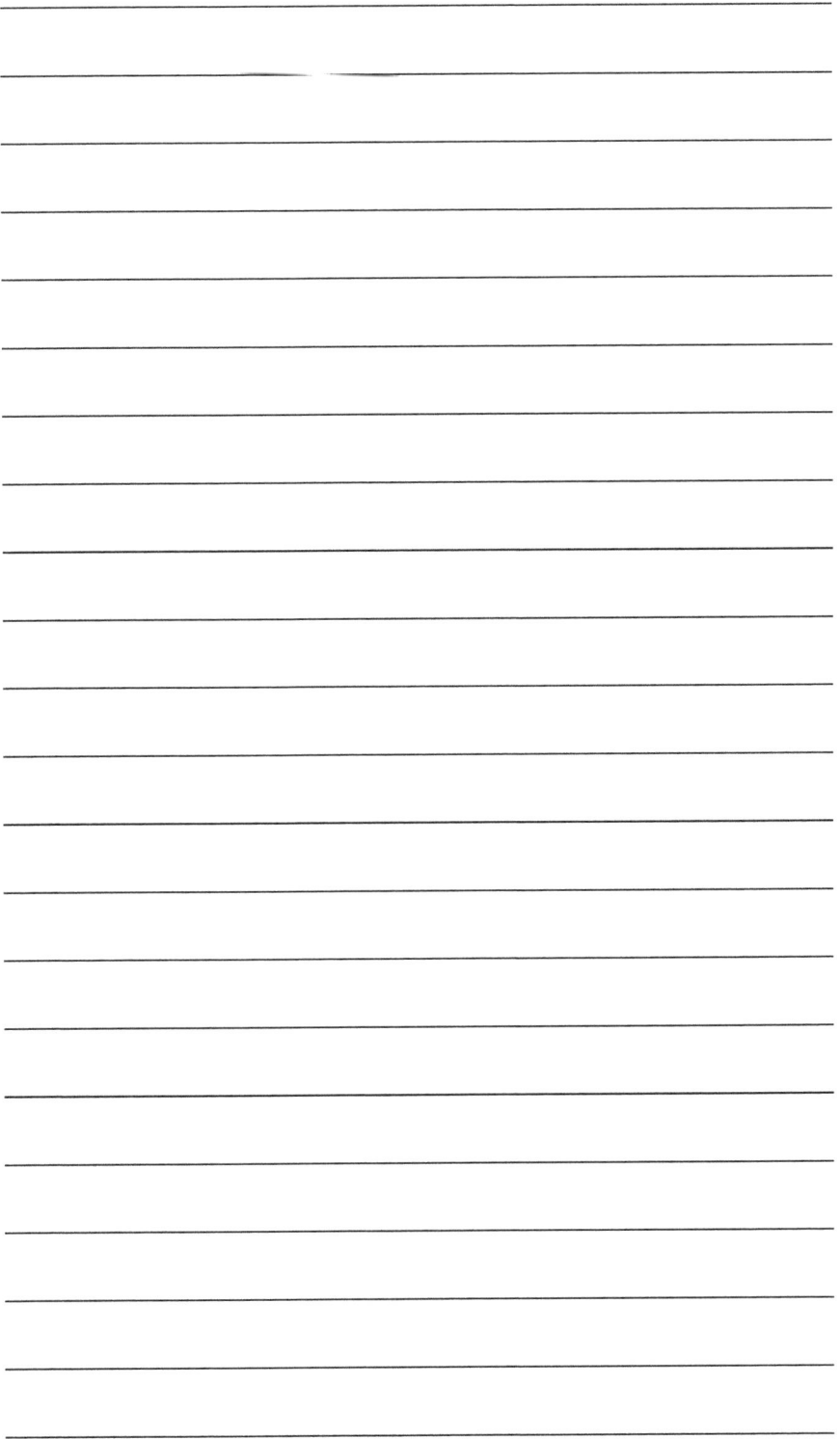

SEEK FIRST THE KINGDOM...

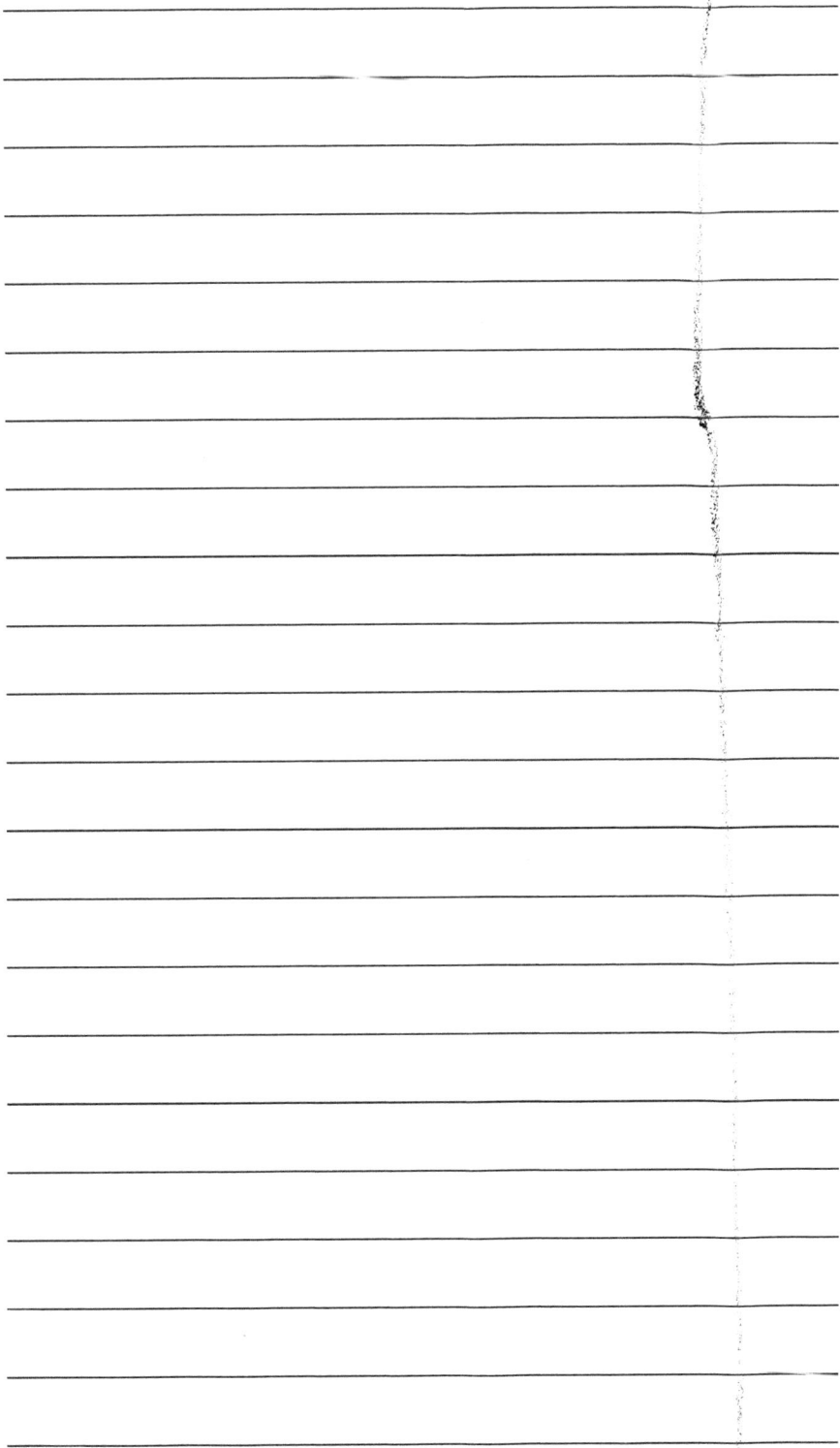

DON'T TURN TO THE RIGHT OR LEFT.

DOUBT YOUR DOUBTS

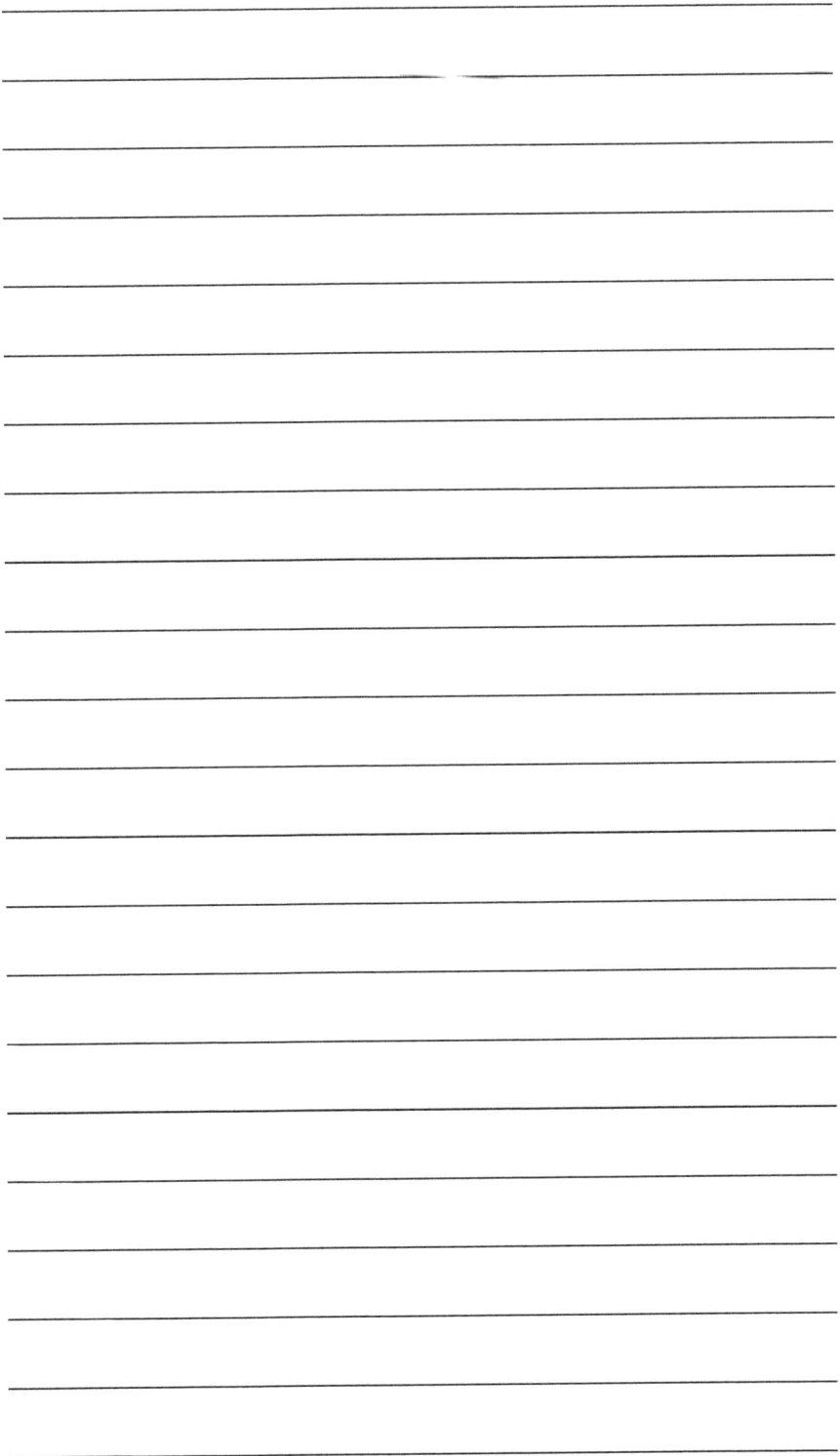

SHHH.
WELL DONE
IS BETTER
THAN WELL SAID.

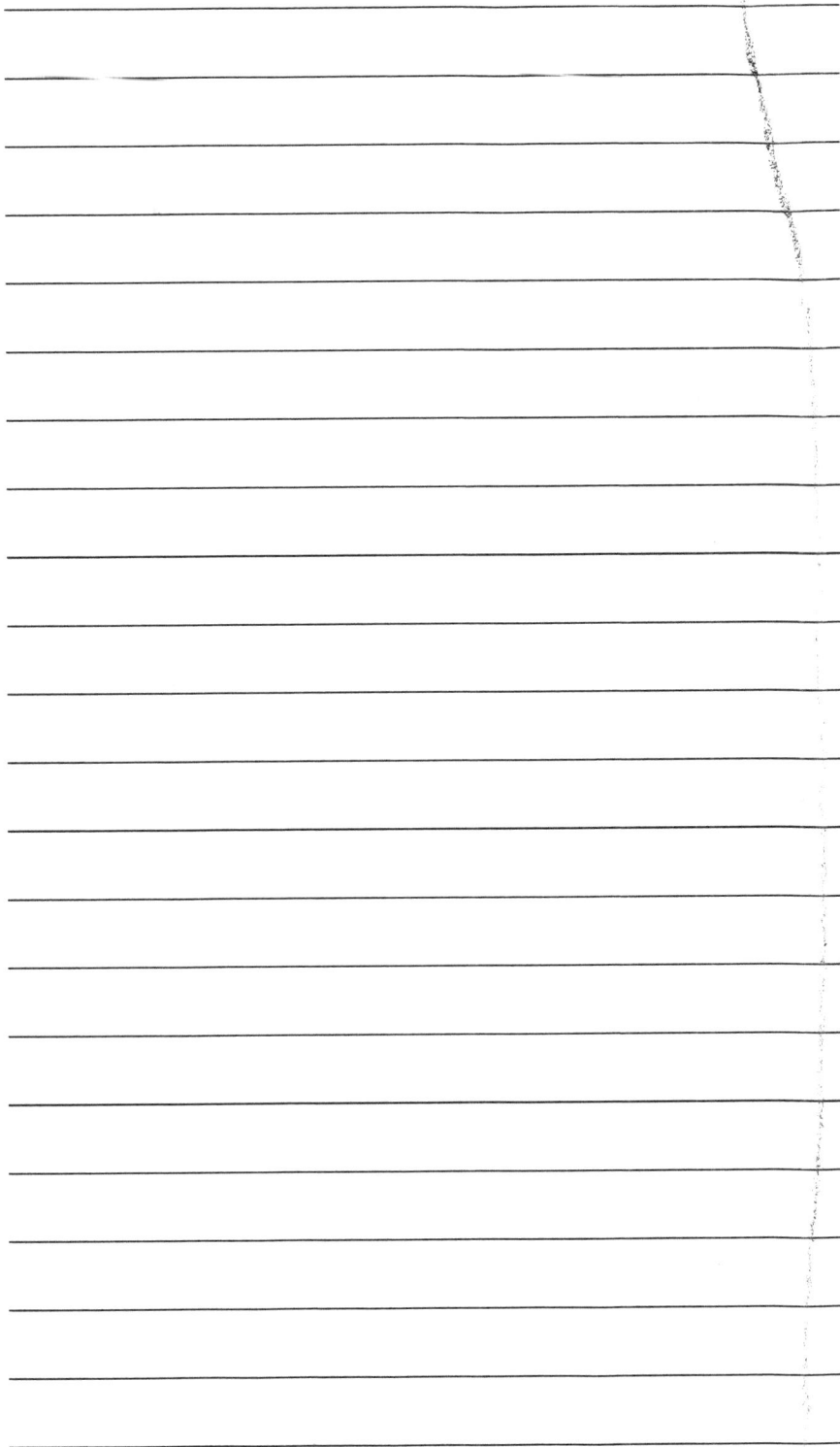

WHAT'S THE LAST THING GOD SAID TO DO?

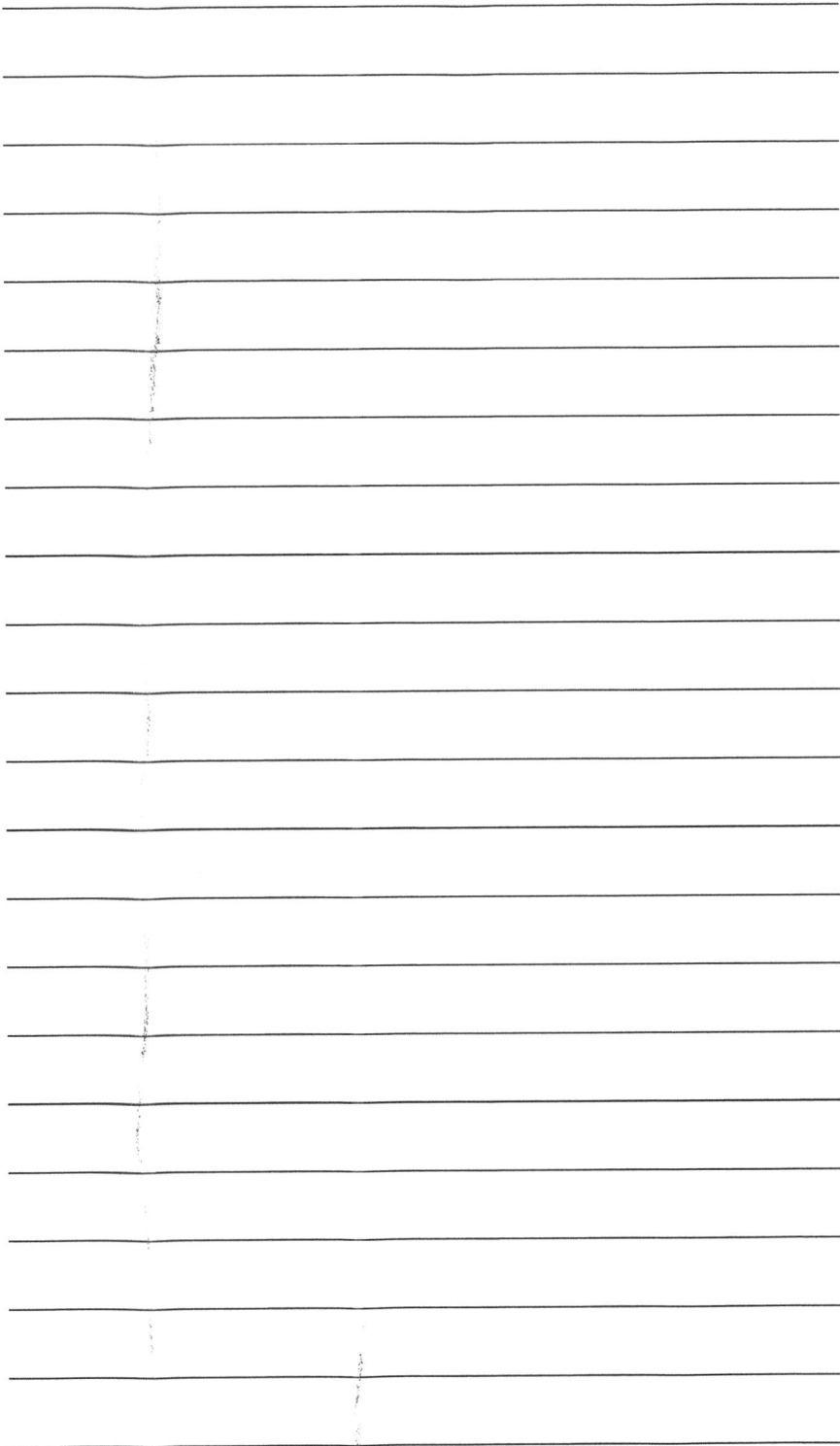

DON'T
GROW
WEARY
IN WELL
DOING.

OBEY ANYWAY.

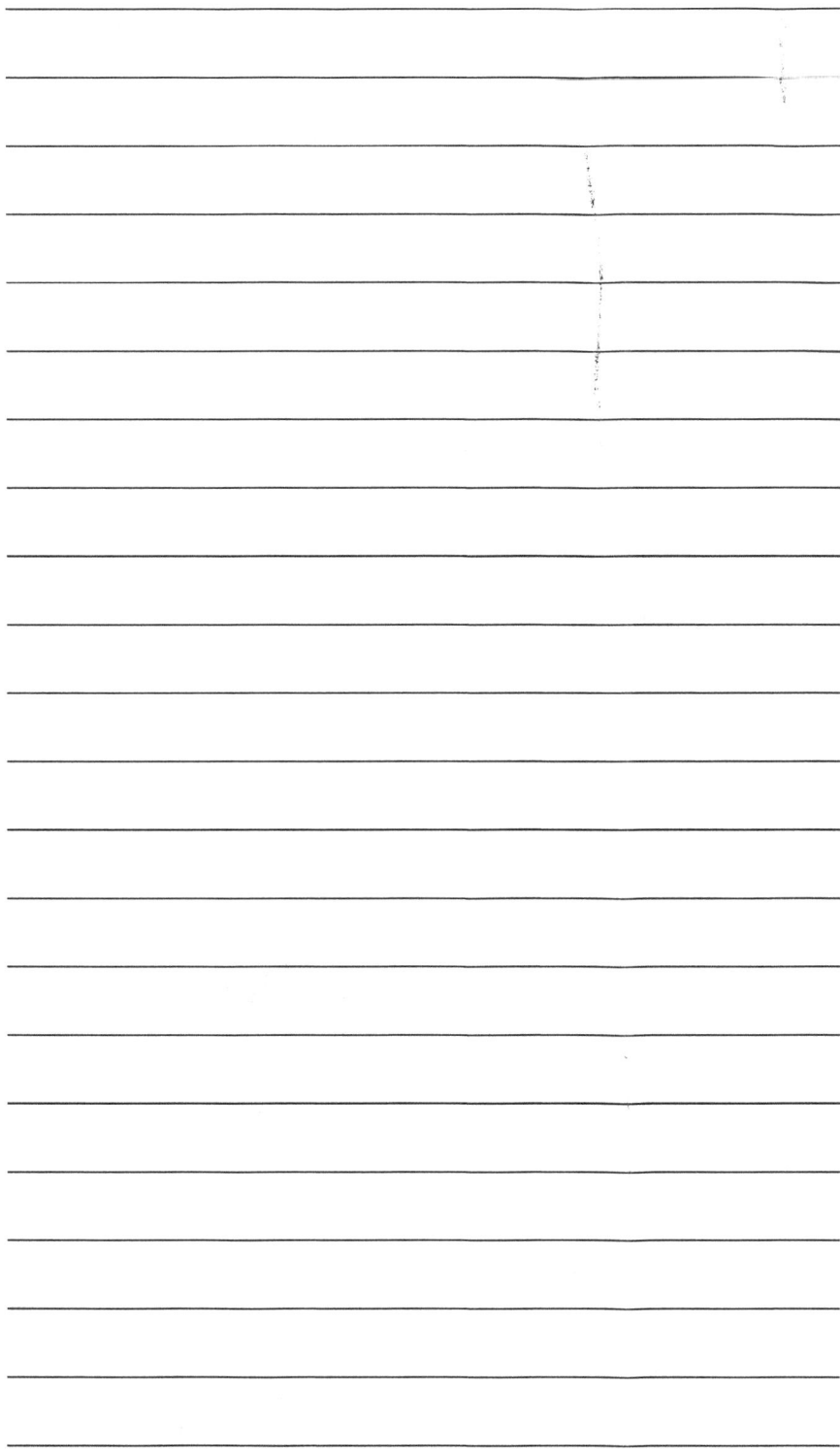

ARE
YOU BEING PRODUCTIVE,
OR JUST BUSY?

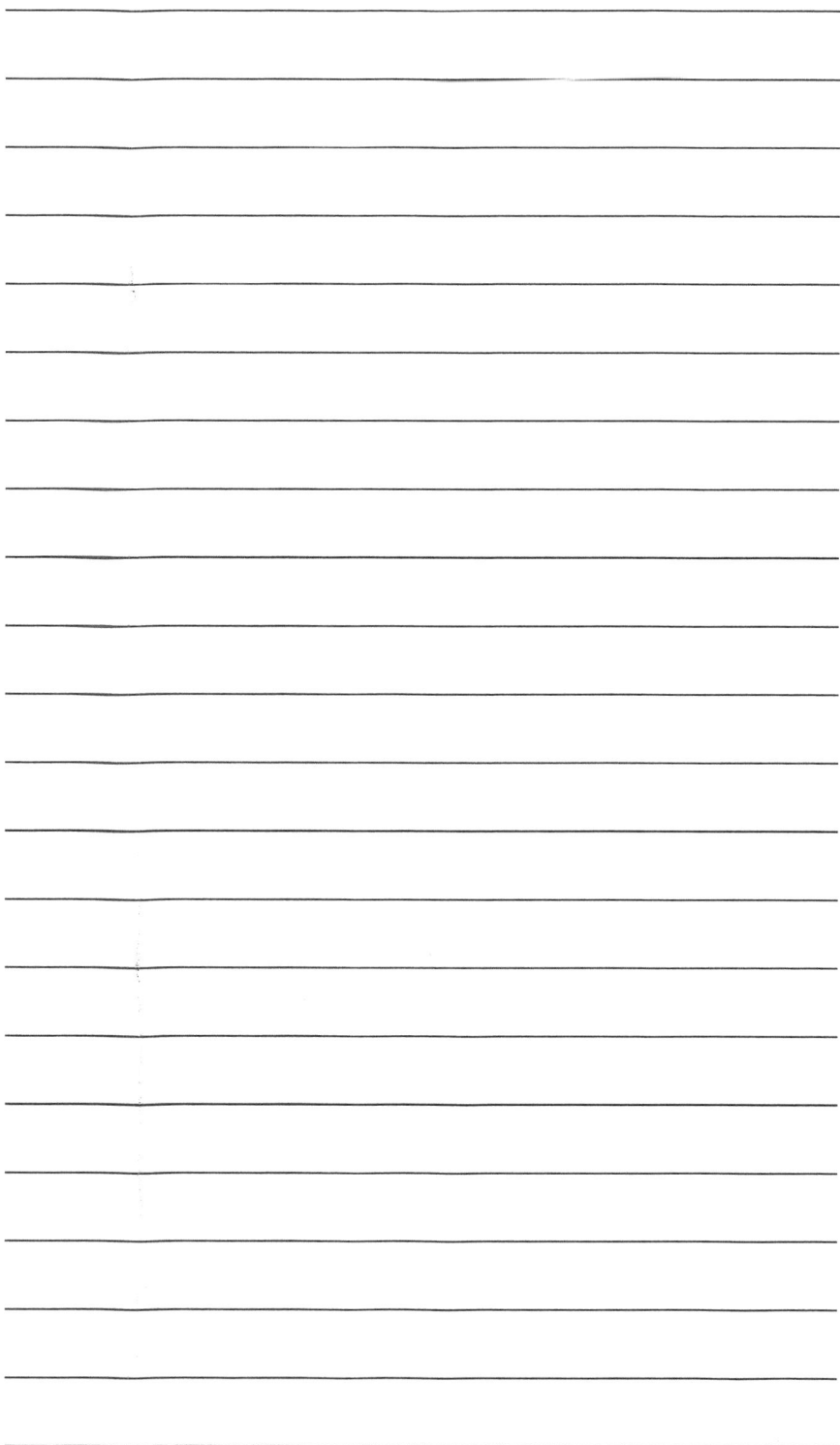

DON'T JUST SURVIVE, THRIVE.

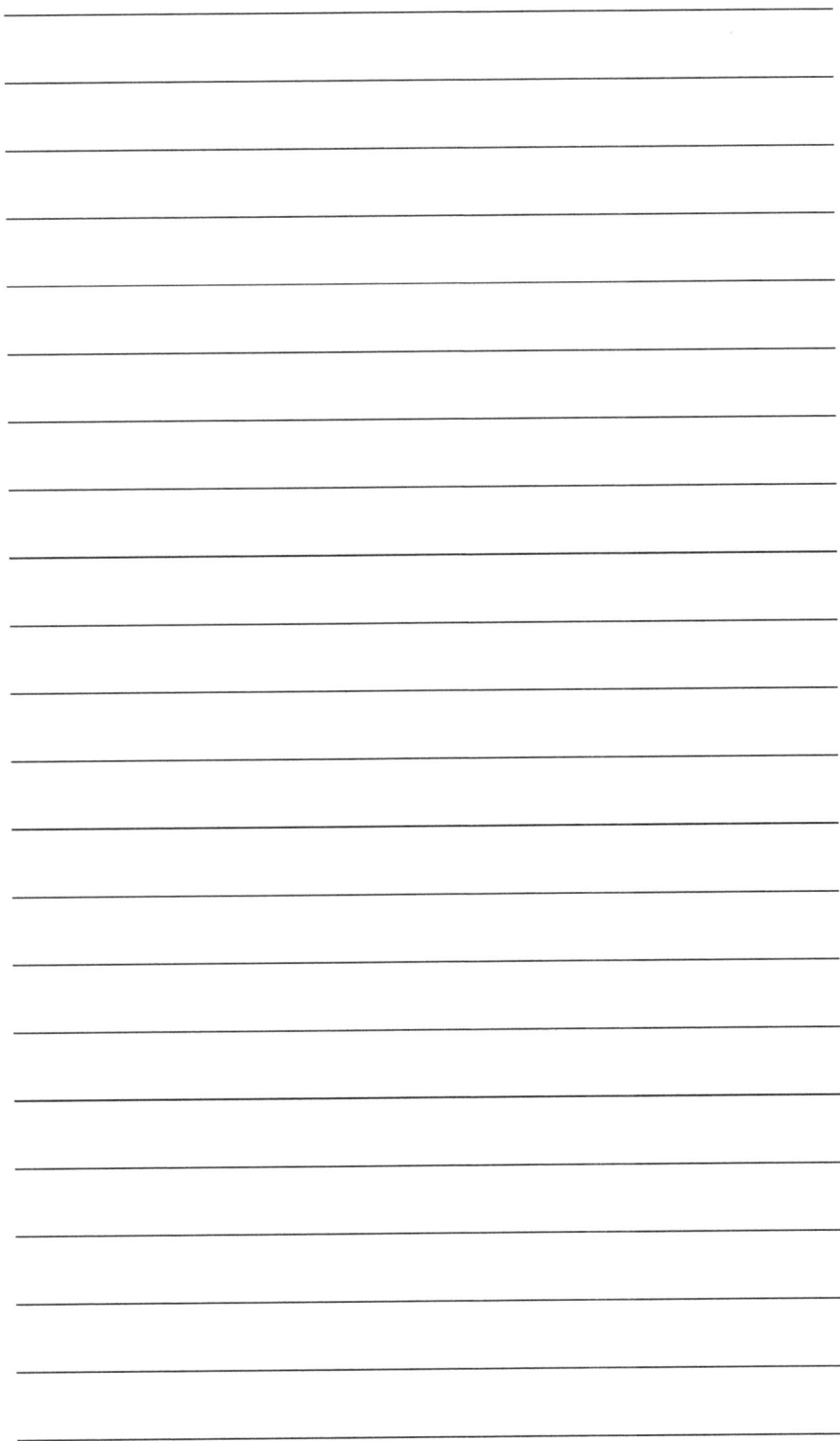

WHO'S SPEAKING, PEER PRESSURE OR PEACE?

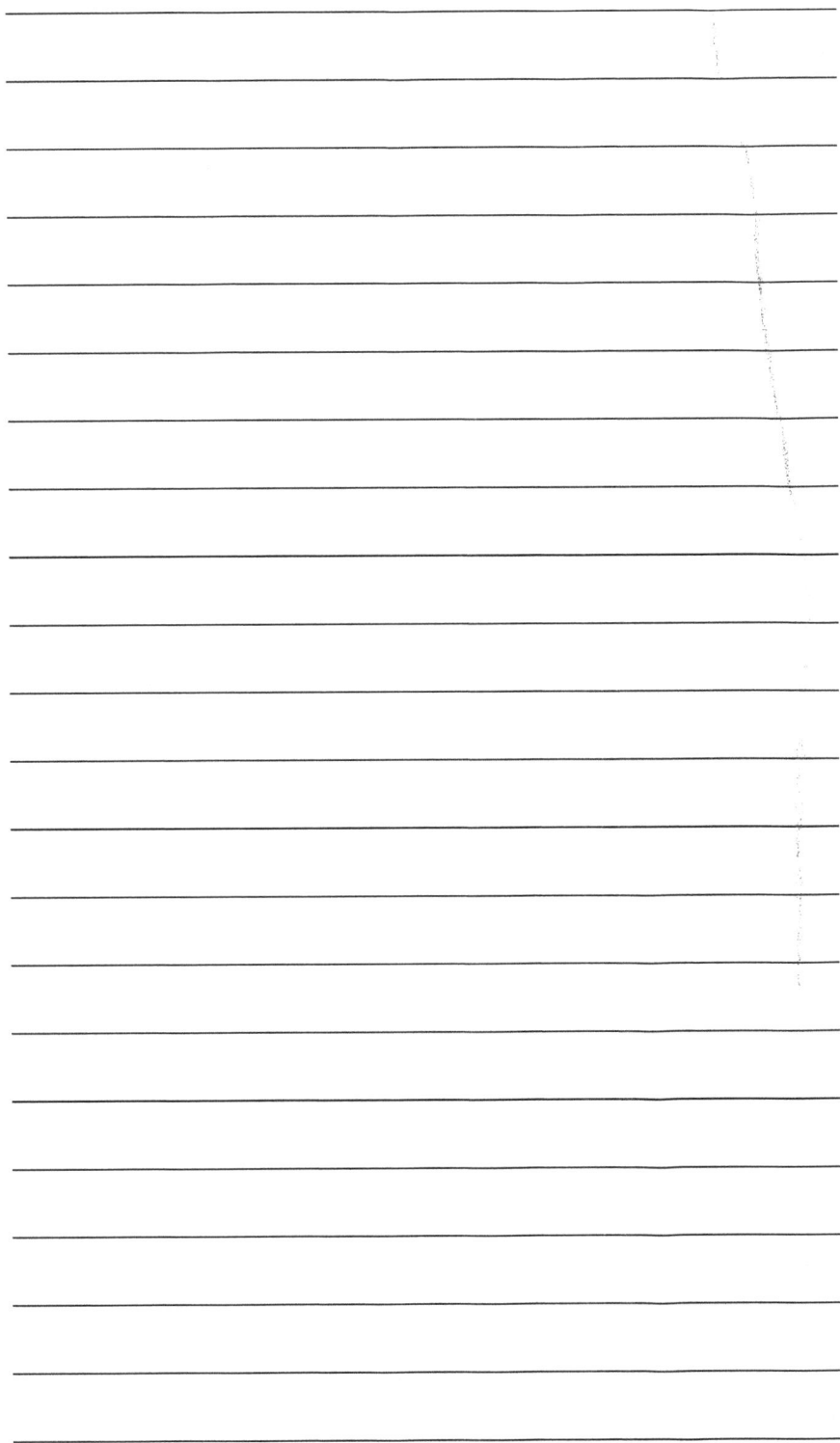

PERMISSION GRANTED, JUST SAY NO.

CHANGE
YOUR
MIND.

WOMEN WHO FINISH

YOU WERE SAVED TO IMPACT YOUR CULTURE. LEAD. SERVE. WIN.
YOUR VOICE WILL SOUND DIFFERENT. DO NOT BLEND IN. STAND OUT.
FOCUS ON YOUR CALLING. IT'S THE ONLY ONE YOU'LL BE GOOD AT.
JUST START. USE YOUR TALENTS. DREAM. ASK. THEN BELIEVE.
YOU WERE GIVEN THE VISION. SO YOU PURSUE IT. DO IT AFRAID.
OBEY. MAKE DISCIPLES. EXPECT THE SUPERNATURAL. EXECUTE.
LAY ONE BRICK TODAY. EXALT CHRIST. THEN GET EXALTED BY GOD.
KNOW YOUR WHY. SOLVE A PROBLEM. MAKE $$. CREATE BEAUTY.
FAIL OFTEN. GRACE WORKS. CHOOSE PROGRESS OVER PERFECTION.

PRIORITIZE YOUR PURPOSE. CELEBRATE YOUR WINS.

BUT FIRST, FINISH.

www.ingramcontent.com/pod-product-compliance
Lightning Source LLC
Chambersburg PA
CBHW060332100426
42812CB00003B/964